THE GREAT APES

THE GREAT APES

First published in the United Kingdom by
Evans Mitchell Books
The Old Forge, 16 Church Street
Rickmansworth, Herts WD3 1DH
United Kingdom

Reprinted March 2009

Photography: copyright © 2007, Cyril Ruoso
Text: copyright © 2007, Emmanuelle Grundmann

Editing: Peter and Gillian Varley
Design: Empriente & Territoires, Paris, France
Pre-press: Studio Goustard, Vanves, France

British Library Cataloguing in Publication
Data. A CIP record of this book is available
on request from the British Library.

ISBN: 978-1-901268-31-7

Printed in Italy

THE GREAT APES

CYRIL RUOSO & EMMANUELLE GRUNDMANN

Evans Mitchell Books

CONTENTS

INTRODUCTION

Great apes have a long history of being either revered or abhorred, according to beliefs, religions, and cultures, and have always been in an ambiguous position: neither really animals any more, nor yet completely human. They occupy a position between nature and culture, monster and animal, bestiality and humanity. In antiquity Aristotle considered them to be intermediate creatures, between animals and men. Later, they were called *Similitudines homini*, almost humans. Everything changed during the Age of Enlightenment: expeditions by naturalists brought the first apes back to Europe, like the chimpanzee offered in 1630 to Frederick Henry, Prince of Orange. Or the little orangutan which arrived in the port of London in 1698, who unfortunately failed to survive the journey but gave rise to the first anatomy lesson on the great ape, given by Dr. Edward Tyson. The zoologist Carl von Linné, father

of modern taxonomy, dared to unite men and apes in one single category and even wanted to go so far as to give man and orangutan the same genus name: *Homo dirunus* for the former and *Homo nocturnes*, or troglodytes, for the latter. But Linné explains, "if I had called man an ape, or vice versa, I should have fallen under the ban of all the ecclesiastics. It may be that as a naturalist, I ought to have done so." The last four decades of research into primatology have chiselled away at the pedestal on which some scientific and religious thinking had placed mankind. It is now an indisputable fact that apes and humans share a common ancestor, and we need at last to get rid of the false belief that *Homo sapiens* descended from apes and that the apes were left behind, further down *Scala naturae*, because they didn't keep up with hominisation and thus failed to become humans. But apes succeeded too, and became today's orangutans, gorillas, bonobos, gibbons and chimpanzees, inhabiting the tropical rainforests of Asia and Africa. Who knows how they will evolve if we let them live in peace. Being an ape is not only a matter of size, although they are the biggest of all primates. Apes also share with humans characteristics such as large brains, extremely high intelligence, the ability to think and plan, an intense and complex social life, tools and technology, warfare, co-operative hunting, and a protracted childhood and longevity. Primatology was a colonial matter, both in Africa and in Indonesia. The great ape's intelligence intrigued observers, and the first studies were experiments such as those on chimpanzees made by Wolfgang Köhler in the Canary islands in the 1920s and at the French chimpanzee school

Pastoria, started in Guinea in 1924, which in the end turned out to be a medical test laboratory. Some early western researchers began studying apes in their natural

environment in the first half of the 20th century, like Richard Lynn Garner, who tried to live in a cage out in the forest in the French Congo in order to observe chimpanzees in 1892, or later Adrian Kortland. But the new primatology, based on long-term field studies, only really began in the 1960s with Toshisada Nishida and Jane Goodall, who both worked on chimpanzees in Tanzania. Their activities led the way to a new vision of the animals, and helped blur the distinction we have put between ourselves and the other animals ever since antiquity. Because apes are so much like us, both genetically (for example, we share with bonobos more than 99% of our DNA), morphologically, cognitively and behaviourally, they can act as a bridge between the two worlds: that of humans and that of other animal species. They can therefore work towards reconciling the western world's still strong Christian belief in

a human-animal dichotomy, which is contrary to that held in Japan. But today, apes are dying and it is one of them, *Homo sapiens sapiens*, who is responsible. One of the main threats to their survival is deforestation, in which we cut, uproot, burn and destroy the emerald forest which is their habitat. Soon, Borneo and Sumatra will be left without any forest, and orangutans will have disappeared. In Africa, the bushmeat trade, logging and war will get the better of the apes and their forests. As our name *Homo sapiens sapiens* indicates so well, we are doubly wise, so, for once, let us be grateful for the name attached to us by scientists – probably incorrectly if we look at human history – and react before it is too late. I hope that future generations will be as fascinated as I am by the apes and their forests, by these cousins who must not end up as mere photographic souvenirs in a family album.

PLANET OF THE APES

At the crack of dawn, as the forest slowly wakes up and the last signs of sleepiness are blown away, a long melancholy duet rises from the canopy and fills the air. Here, in the dense tropical rainforest of Borneo, two species of gibbon share the upper strata of this multi-layered ecosystem. Gibbons and their siamang relatives belong to the lesser apes. Although they show the main characteristics of apes, they are the smallest on the family tree and the first to have diverged from its main branch. From India to

or greyish. In other species, such as the white-handed gibbon, the colouring varies from cream to black, but this time it is independent of gender or age. Behaving like trapeze artists, gibbons and siamangs use their elongated arms and hook-like hands to swing from branch to branch, crossing the forest in search of the fruits and leaves they feed on. When their morning concert comes to an end, I cannot but admit, as I sit under the tree where they are performing, that they are the most elegant and artistic of all apes.

Gibbons and siamangs

China, through Burma, Indonesia and Thailand, eleven species of Hylobatidae inhabit the dense forests of south-east Asia. The largest of all, and probably the loudest singer – no doubt a tenor chorister – is the siamang, stockily built and wearing a long silky black fur coat featuring a scrotal tuft resembling a short tail. In the early morning, after the other gibbons have finished their own song, siamangs begin their astonishing concert, using their inflated throat sac as a resonance chamber: the male more or less screaming while the female produces a series of barks. Some species display an interesting, and for primates unusual, sexual dimorphism, or difference in appearance, as the two sexes can have their own distinctive fur colouration. Male golden-cheeked, Chinese white-cheeked, black and pileated gibbons are black, whereas the females are golden to buff

An orange shadow glides through the exuberant vegetation. Discreet and silent as ever, an orangutan has just passed by. Known as mawas in Sumatra, and maiass or kahiyu in Borneo, this man of the forest is at ease in the tree-top world. This canopy ape, the largest tree-living or arboreal mammal, rarely descends to the ground, except for the large adult males, whose 80kgs allow them to roam without danger on the dry land. Although they have long disappeared from Borneo, tigers still pace the undergrowth of the

Sumatran and Bornean orangutans

Sumatran rainforest waiting to ambush prey such as careless, young orangutans. The soil here swarms with parasites, and primatologists have found that, although orangutans sometimes fall and suffer fractures, these heal fast and they catch fewer colds and other diseases than other more terrestrial apes. Because of the genetic distance between the two types of red-haired ape living on the islands of Borneo and Sumatra, scientists have now separated them into two distinct species, according to the island they live on. The Sumatran has lighter, denser and longer fur, a narrower face and a more slender appearance than its neighbour from Borneo. Apart from these differences, males from both species exhibit a broad moon-face thanks to their flabby cheek pads. This attribute probably plays a double role, both to attract females and as a means of directing

the ape's long and energetic call in a particular direction. A throat sac adds to the power of these bellowing calls, which are carried as far as a kilometre and give a clear message to other adult males: "keep off my territory and females". Nomadic and somehow solitary, orangutans lead a life in slow motion, encouraged by their size and preference for heights. A way of life that may be summarised as feed and travel – travel and feed. To exploit their arboreal environment to its fullest, they have developed a four-handed technique that enables them to reach the thinner outer branches of the tree crowns, while spreading their entire weight over several branches – a must for one who likes juicy fruits! This arboreal athlete shows a predilection for extractive foraging, and is far from being the dunce of the ape family, as it was once described.

Behind the image of a brutal beast, kidnapping and raping women, conveyed by King Kong and other films, there is actually a gentle vegetarian giant, sitting in his pantry longing for nettles or a handful of forest fruits. Most scientists now recognize two distinct species of gorilla, separated from one another by the inner Congo Basin, and each including two subspecies: the western gorilla (*Gorilla gorilla*) and the eastern gorilla (*Gorilla berengei*). While all live in lowland rainforests, *Gorilla berengei berengei*, a sub-species of the eastern gorilla and the most famous of them, has made his home in the mountainous areas of the Virungas and the impenetrable Bwindi forests, where rain and mist come and go amongst the bamboos, gigantic lobelias and fragrant celery. A giant among apes, the male gorilla can weigh up to 160kgs compared with only a mere 70kgs

Mountain and lowland gorillas

for the female. Adult males are either silverbacks, if they lead a harem, or blackbacks, when they do not yet have access to females for reproduction. Display and showing off – such as chest beating – are essential to impress potential rivals and keep them away from the females.
In gorilla etiquette, the individuals seldom come to blows and even intimidatory charges usually stop right in front of the adversary's nose.

Chimpanzees

Dragging a huge log behind him, Yolo, a young adult male, hair erect, shows off in an intimidation display. Seeing these 50 to 60kgs of muscle at work, I make myself as small as I can, crouching in the vegetation, hoping it is a good enough sign of allegiance and submission. And indeed it must have been convincing. As suddenly as it all began, Yolo swaps his Mr Hyde role for Dr Jekyll and heads quietly back to his group, further west in the little forest overlooking the village of Bossou in Guinea. Chimpanzees are indeed quite impressive and the males easily become angry. Although they are covered with a black coat like the other African apes, their hairless faces and large ears are pinkish, often dotted with ginger-coloured spots. As infants, chimpanzees' backsides have a small white hair tuft, which slowly disappears as they become adult. Found in 21 African countries throughout the tropical zone, they are highly social, skilful toolmakers, organised hunters, formidable politicians and occasional warriors, but also experts in reconciliation just like another species of great apes: *Homo sapiens*, with whom chimpanzees share 98.6% of their DNA.

With a neat and almost too wise haircut, parted in the middle and accompanied by side whiskers, the ebony bonobo is undoubtedly the most graceful ape. Also called the pygmy chimpanzee, even though there is nothing pygmy about it other than its name, it is slightly more slender and darker than its closest cousin, the common chimpanzee. Having been confused with the chimpanzee for a long time, the bonobo was only discovered and described in 1929, by the German anatomist Ernst Schwartz, who was intrigued by a skull in Belgium's Tervuren Museum which was too small to be that of a chimpanzee. Bonobos are found only in a small enclave of regularly-flooded forest in the northern part of the Democratic Republic of the Congo (DRC), and do not co-exist with other apes. The area is demarcated by the Congo river in the north, the Kasai river in the south and the Lualaba river in the east. It was the front zone of a country at war for many years, an irony for this ape, with its somewhat hippie

Bonobos

life, following the slogan "make love not war". Indeed sex is a dominating element in the lives of bonobos, as they usually substitute love for violence in their conflict resolutions. Sex is the cement of their social life, although rude and aggressive behaviour can be displayed in an encounter with a non-related group. More intriguing and unusual in primate society, power here is in the hands of the females, who rule and take decisions for the group. Bonobos feed on fruits, various herbaceous plants, honey and mushrooms, with sometimes a handful of insects, but unlike their chimpanzee cousins they do not hunt or eat meat. With their stature and often upright stance when walking, bonobos look very much like our Australopithecus ancestors. Genetically they are our closest relatives as we share more or less 99.6% of genes, but bonobos are also the most irresistible of apes.

Guinea

Sierra Leone

Liberia   Ghana   Nigeria

Ivory Coast   Cameroon

   Equatorial Guinea

    Gabon

People's Republic of the Congo

Central African Republic

Uganda

Rwanda

Burundi

Democratic Republic of the Congo

Tanzania

Chimpanzee

Bonobo

Lowland gorilla

Mountain gorilla

A PUZZLING FAMILY TREE

China

India

Bangladesh

Myanmar

Thaïland

Laos

Vietnam

Cambodia

Malaysia

Sumatra

Borneo

Indonesia

Java

Gibbon and siamang

Bornean orangutan

Sumatran orangutan

The evolution of both Hominoid and Hominid looks like an unfinished puzzle, in which most of the pieces are missing and where one can only make hypotheses, using evidence and a pinch of imagination to compose the overall picture. Nevertheless we have some clues from fossil discoveries that help us understand the family tree better. Apes used to reign over the African forests at the beginning of the Miocene period, around 23 to 20 million years ago, before expanding into Europe and Asia. But around 15 million years ago Cercopithecoids began to emerge, and their small size and less fussy attitude to food enabled them to occupy many new ecological niches. Between 8 and 5 million years ago global climate warming pushed shrinking tropical forests further towards the equator and the expansion of Cercopithecoids signalled the decline of Hominoids. Because apes were dependent on the canopy many species began to be in trouble, and the only way to survive was to follow some of the Cercopithecoids onto the ground and exploit new opportunities; this is what the ancestors of chimpanzees probably did. Others, such as the ancestors of the gorilla, opted to specialise in eating highly fibrous foods, while Sivapithecus and later orangutans almost certainly concentrated on extractive foraging, exploiting hard food and certainly nuts. Today, the questions surrounding the last common ancestor of chimpanzees and humans, and the timing of the divergence between the two lineages, still remain. In 2006, four geneticists showed that humans and chimpanzees separated not 8, 9 or 10, but 6.3 million years ago. Not a big difference for primatologists, who suspected this long ago due to the behavioural similarities observed in humans and modern apes, but important for palaeontologists whose star fossils – Toumaï or Orrorin – changed from being the oldest human examples to those of "mere apes". Today, ape distribution reflects not only ecological changes but also human influence. Although most ape species have declined in number, one has succeeded in all possible environments. But this single species carries a heavy burden, as it is responsible for the extermination of its own family members.

Frans de Waal, C. H. Candler Professor of Primate Behavior at Emory University, and director of the Living Links Centre in Atlanta, says that "humans changed more over evolutionary time than did apes. We began walking upright, developed a larger brain, and lost body hair. Ape evolution did not stand still though, but they remained closer to their ancestral environment, the forest, while our ancestors gradually left it to enter the savannah. If the habitat of origin was rain-forest, the ape with the least reason to change might have been the bonobo, who never left it. They may therefore represent the most ancestral type. We can hope that genetic analyses will help us decide whether the last common ancestor was bonobo-like or perhaps more chimpanzee-like. This makes a huge difference, given that bonobos are relatively peaceful and female-dominated, while chimpanzees are aggressive, more territorial, and male-dominated."

Hominoid family tree

Lar gibbon — Hylobates lar

Sumatran orangutan — Pongo abelii

Mountain gorilla — Gorilla beringei

Chimpanzee

Bonobo — Pan troglodytes, Pan paniscus

Man

Hylobatidae

Ponginae

Gorillinae

Pongidae

Paninae

Hominoidea	Hominidae	Homininae	Homo sapiens
Superfamily	Family	Sub-family	Genus & species

Sumatran rainforests contain a treasure trove of over 10,000 species of plants, 200 species of mammals, 580 of birds, a cohort of insects and other vertebrates. Lianas are abundant and cling on the large buttress-tree trunks while others, such as *Tetrastigma*, host the parasitic *Rafflesia arnoldii*, the biggest flower in the world.

moist and dark Indonesian Borneo rainforest, the land of the red ape. These tropical forests, along with those in Sumatra, are most unusual since they exhibit a unique asynchrony of flowering and fruiting, both in time and space. Here is found a family of trees called Dipterocarps, giants of their kind, that have evolved a unique method of deceiving seed predators, using mast-fruiting episodes which usually reflect the El Niño southern climate oscillation. The amount of fruit in both Borneo and Sumatra varies greatly, and mast-fruiting times alternate with periods of fruit shortage every four to seven years. During cornucopia times, animals gorge themselves with seeds and fruits, but leave enough seeds to regenerate the forest. In other years, they have to content themselves with leaves, figs, bark and a few

Mast fruiting episodes vs fruit shortage ones in Borneo and Sumatra

Accompanied by a long, misty veil, the orange sun rises slowly above the still monochromatic forest. Slowly the bluish drowsiness gives way to an explosion of vibrant colours and sounds reverberating through the canopy. The six o'clock cicadas announce the relief of the night shift. In the air and on the ground a swarm of creatures awakes, and like a super-organism gives life to the forest cathedral. A brief moment of coolness and the day star establishes its authority with a swiftness that is always surprising, and chases away the night. Here we are, plunging into the heart of the

other fruit species. This is the case with orangutans, and primatologists have found that occasional gorging with high-calorie fruit has a direct impact on the ape's social life. The abundance of calories leads to higher female oestrogen levels and a more active mating period. In contrast, during periods of fruit shortage, calorie intake drops and apes begin to produce ketones, chemical compounds indicating that the orangutans are burning their own fat reserves for energy. Primates have always maintained a long-

lasting and intimate relationship with trees and forests. Trees offer food and lodging, and in return primates help pollinate them and disperse their seeds, embracing the role of the gardener of this gigantic edible forest. In this organic self-service supermarket, both orangutans and chimpanzees have a menu of 200 to 300 plant species and plant parts to choose from. Mountain gorillas pick from about 150 plant species and their lowland cousins from around 100. Plants are even more generous than that, as they also offer a first-aid cupboard. In 1989, primatologist Michael Huffman and his Tanzanian assistant

described an unusual and exceptional behaviour: one of the Mahale chimpanzees, known to suffer from intestinal disorders, was seen plucking the stem of the bitter *Vernonia amygdalina* plant, which is usually avoided. Soon afterwards the individual recovered. In Gombe and Kibale, chimpanzees were using leaves of *Aspilia*, but in a different manner. Whereas *Vernonia* acts chemically, *Aspilia* helps get rid of intestinal parasites mechanically. The leaf of this relative of the sunflower is carefully folded like origami in the chimpanzee's mouth, and gulped down unchewed. The surface of the leaf is covered

Trees provide both food and aerial highways to cross gaps in the canopy. Brachiation, swinging or climbing is used by the arboreal orangutans who rarely come down to the ground, except for large flanged adult males such as this one.

with hair and as it passes through the digestive tract it traps worms, acting like Velcro. The use of several plant species with medicinal properties – either leaves or fruits – by chimpanzees, bonobos and gorillas has already been recorded. To find food sources, a detailed mental map is needed to locate all the food trees, and particularly in the case of orangutans and gibbons an awareness of their fruiting periods. But a wide network of roads, paths and routes is also needed. Gorillas in the lowlands can use the elephant highways and other animal-made tunnels through the dense undergrowth of

vegetation. Arboreal apes have an invaluable
ally in the lianas: thin or thick, smooth or
twisted, these link trees together, providing
plant 'wires' on which they hang, swing,
climb and sway. Gibbons are true trapezists,
almost flying between branches and lianas.
This has led, through evolution, to
a reduction of the gibbon's thumb and
eventually to its hand having four elongated
fingers and a tiny thumb, which functions
as a hook to grab the branches and lianas
while in flight. Orangutans are not so much

Vines and lianas form wildlife highways through the canopy

In the mist of the Rwanda
mountain forest, in an
astonishing landscape
where one would not be
surprised to see elves
and goblins appear
behind a mossy trunk,
lives the gorilla, the
largest of all apes.

trapezists as skilled balancers or equilibrists, performing a slightly less spectacular aerial act but one which is nevertheless impressive considering their weight. They know how to use their heavy bodies and transform what could be a handicap into an asset. To cross a branch- and liana-free space, they climb up small flexible trunks to the point where

Life in a 3-dimensional tree-top world

these begin to bend beneath the ape's weight. Then, with their arms and long hands outstretched, they transmit a swinging movement to the small tree until, with their hands held out, they can grab leaves and then twigs and eventually a branch. Although chimpanzees and bonobos spend a variable amount of time in trees, they are expert climbers, but on the ground prefer to travel in Indian file. As for gorillas, their weight is a handicap for arboreal travel and they feel more at ease on the ground. However, young and adolescent gorillas enjoy playing in the three-dimensional, tree-top world, and adult lowland gorillas frequently climb trees in search of fruits.

Mountain gorillas live in a gigantic larder filled with nettles, thistles, wild celery, lobelias and bamboos. Each day, they eat up to 30kgs of vegetation.

Building a nest to sleep in is a daily task but from time to time, a chimpanzee can also rearrange an old nest for his siesta or a long, sound night's sleep. Young chimpanzees like to transform lianas into gymnastic apparatus.

Trees also provide lodgings, some becoming apartment buildings when night falls and a group of chimpanzees or bonobos begins to build nests in them. All apes apart from gibbons and siamangs build nests to sleep and rest in each day. These are made after they have carefully chosen a suitable site, at a branch fork for example, or on top of a tree crown for those who want a nest with a view. Then the ape bends the branches, folding them and making a comfortable

mattress, eventually adding other leafy branches cut nearby. It seems that individual preferences can sometimes be observed, as I did once while following orangutans. One male, named Luther, always favoured the broad and rather tough leaves of ironwood, while others kept choosing tiny, narrow,

As he makes his leafy bed, so he must lie on it

rounded leaves. Even more interestingly, some red ape populations emit a so-called 'raspberry' vocalisation, but they do so before beginning to build their overnight

Apes such as this bonobo and chimpanzees live in a three-dimensional world and know the location and fruiting periods of each tree thanks to a complex mental map.

bed in northern Borneo, or after the task is
finished in Sumatra. This socially transmitted
behaviour may represent a cultural variation
in the orangutan population, according to
some scientists. Amongst bonobos,
the primatologist Barbara Fruth has shown
that the social structure of the group affects

the choice of nesting site; females usually
nest close to each other, while males
choose sites on the periphery of the female
cluster. If rain begins to pour down,
orangutans often cover their nests with
a leafy and waterproof roof. Being so large
and heavy, adult gorillas, especially

mountain ones, build ground nests, wide beds filled with squashed vegetation that insulates them from the cold and damp floor. Nests are a very interesting artefact, which is widely present in the animal kingdom although mostly used for breeding purposes – a safe place where the brood is cared for. They are less common among primates, and are used more as a place of safety and for sleeping. Apart from some prosimians – the most primitive extant primates, like the aye-aye – only great apes build these leafy nests and some primatologists argue that such sleeping platforms were used by early Hominids such as Australopithecines. Nest building is quite complex and requires a technique which is largely acquired through learning. It takes a few years for a young ape to master it and build a proper, functional nest. Until then, he sleeps huddled up to his mother in her nest.

Everyone sleeps apart but females with young share a bed with a view

Young bonobos like this one living at Lola Ya Bonobo, will have to learn which are the edible plants in their environment – they do this mostly by observing their mother and the other adults in their group.

Male orangutans, polygynous, live in a large home range of around five square kilometres overlapping the ranges of several females. Males come to meet and mate with females briefly when they are sexually receptive. Raising the offspring is left to the mother.

It was one of those rainy days, with a drizzle that pierces you right through and chills you to the bone after a few hours. In the distance, mounts Karisimbi, Mikeno and Visoke seem to be shrouded in a thick mist, like the one in the film that made some bluish glinted fur gorillas famous. A gust of wind suddenly blows the fog away, and in an amphitheatre of vegetation 39 gorillas appear. This is the Susa group, unusual among gorillas as it contains three silver-backs, when one is the rule in this species. Gorillas live in true harems composed of one fully adult male, the silverback, surrounded with up to five adult females and their young. One might ask why such primates choose to live in groups, when others such as gibbons choose monogamy or, like orangutans, solitary lives. What contribution does social life make, and what are the real costs and

benefits of such a way of life?

Primate social life reflects its environment, its constraints and most specifically the availability of food, but it is also linked to the primate's size and appetite. Vegetarian mountain gorillas live among a vegetable bonanza where there is absolutely no food restriction that might prevent gregariousness. But why do some primates inhabiting the same environment live in groups, like crab-eating macaques in Sumatra or the Thomas langurs, while orangutans are solitary and siamangs enjoy life in couples? Apes are the biggest of the primates and

If chimpanzees exhibit complex greeting and reconciliation rituals, bonobos are sex-addicts when it comes to reinforcing the bonds of the group. Others, such as gibbons and orangutans, are more vocal, living too far apart for gesture-based communication.

The prolonged and frequent œstrus in female bonobos results in lowering the pressure and aggression between males to gain access to them.

therefore much less sensitive to predation than monkeys. However competition for food is stronger because of their large size, and apes therefore tend to live in smaller groups; this can be seen in its simplest form in Asian apes, and is sometimes quite variable timewise, for example among chimpanzees leading a so-called fission-fusion social life, where members of a community form temporary parties, small subsets of the whole group, re-unite, and then separate into sub-groups again.

It's all a matter of food availability

The asynchrony displayed by Dipterocarp trees, an important food source for the orangutans in Borneo and Sumatra, has been the driving force towards a solitary life for the red ape, as primatologist Carel van Schaik has shown. Indeed, when food sources are more abundant and evenly distributed in time and space, as in the Suaq swamps in Sumatra, orangutans tend to congregate; they associate, travel in a group, and co-ordinate their movements in order to stay together. This is a quite different picture from Borneo, where the red ape is more reclusive and doesn't spend more than 5% of its time associating with its peers.

So are they solitary or not? Orangutans are indeed social animals, as choosing to be solitary is also considered as social behaviour. They show a more or less gregarious way of life, depending on the environmental constraints, but probably keep in touch permanently with others. There are still mysteries to be solved if we are to understand the social habits of the red hermit

Real politicians, chimpanzees form alliances and master the coup d'etat, like these males living at the Vallée des Singes in France, who have jointly decided to defeat the alpha male.

better. Pant-hoots ring out in the forest, breathy calls whose pitch starts low and rises. A muffled drumming on tree trunks seems to echo the first sound, further

Although infrequent and rare, deadly fights sometimes occur between male orangutans. This Bornean orangutan has arrested development of his secondary sexual characteristics, as a flanged male lives in the vicinity.

Coalitions, alliances and coups d'état: that's chimpanzee politics

to the east. We are in the Taï forest, in Ivory Coast, and chimpanzees are on the move. They live in a fission-fusion social structure like the bonobos. This allows the apes flexibility in exploiting patchy food resources, a strategy all the more attractive since chimpanzees have few predators in the forest. But contests between males, to gain access to females and hence to

*Professor **Carel van Schaik**, Director of the Anthropological Institute and Museum at the University of Zurich, says that "orangutans are, to some extent, an ape of paradox: in many areas they hardly group at all, but in Suaq they regularly do. By living closer together, orangutans gain social benefits such as play time and opportunities to observe others performing special techniques. We think that even though they tend to be mainly solitary, there is probably more contact among individuals than we used to think: when they meet, it is clearly not random. My guess is that they use auditory cues a lot, to know the whereabouts of each other. We often see them listening very carefully. They definitely have some form of local communities, in which some neighbours are more appreciated than others."*

Be the strongest or cheat to win females' favour

reproduction, are another competitive factor in addition to the competition for food. Male gorillas beat their chests in an imposing display, drag logs and vocalise loudly to impress potential rivals, while male orangutans, gibbons and siamangs sing to assert their territorial boundaries to wandering competitors. In chimpanzees, it is a matter of politics. For each sex group two hierarchies

Once he is at the head of a harem, the male gorilla has to face very little competition for females from other males. And if a bachelor comes too close, a touch of bluff and a loud intimidatory display will do the trick.

co-exist in the community. While females inherit the rank of their mothers, as this is a matrilineal system, each male has to fight to gain a rank important enough to put him in a favourable position in the quest for sex. Males form coalitions, and enter into alliances with powerful high-ranking females.

The stronger, the better, but less robust males can find themselves a place in the sun through trickery, like Mike, not really a bodybuilder but full of ideas. This young male chimpanzee invented a new display technique by grabbing two empty kerosene tanks left near the research camp in Gombe

National Park; holding one in each hand, sometimes even three, he would run and charge towards the group with the tins clattering ahead of him. This strategy, observed by primatologist Jane Goodall in 1964, enabled Mike to intimidate his rivals so effectively that he succeeded in rising

from a very low position in the hierarchy to become the alpha male in a few months. But, as primatologist Frans de Waal puts it, "if the chimpanzee resolves sexual issues with power, the bonobo resolves power issues with sex". Unlike chimpanzee communities, where females form the social

Emigrating to avoid inbreeding and incest

core of the group and males leave their birthplaces on maturity in order to avoid incest and inbreeding, the situation is the opposite among the bonobos. Here females migrate to new groups but although resident males are closely related to each other, they do not form organised alliances like female chimpanzees. Moreover, females develop a network of alliances amongst themselves, even though they are unrelated to each other, and they stick together if a male threatens. This female co-operation may have evolved to counter the potential threat of infanticide, never yet observed

Sexual selection – the contest between adult males to be the most attractive to females – has contributed during the apes' evolution to male gorillas and orangutans being almost twice the size of females.

in bonobos but found in mountain gorillas. Not only do females emigrate and co-operate, they also hold the reins of government in the community, especially when it comes to food. Chimpanzee males, particularly high-ranking ones, let the females eat only when their own appetite is satisfied. Among

How to enter the mating game if you're an orangutan

bonobos, females feed together, take turns and rarely compete but easily trade food for sex, as I have often witnessed in the free-ranging community of the Lola ya Bonobo sanctuary. Among male orangutans a hierarchy also exists, but sub-adult, or unflanged, males who were previously thought to be left out of the mating game have developed an alternative strategy. Although their secondary sexual characteristics can sometimes fail to develop for up to 20 years after reaching sexual maturity, these arrested males are fertile, sexually active and can sire offspring. But their presence in a female's territory is not welcomed by fully developed males, who jealously guard their females. However, primatologist Sri Suci Utami has shown that about half of the offspring can be attributed to unflanged males and that

flanged males do not have a reproductive monopoly. Although arrested males are not always welcomed by female Bornean orangutans, in Sumatra we regularly see females engage in durable relationships with them. This could be an investment for the future, when these males will have become dominant and fully-developed. As Sri Suci Utami explains, male orangutans have developed two alternative strategies: sitting, calling and waiting in the case of flanged males, and actively going out, searching and finding their mates by unflanged ones.

Play and sex seem to be key to the bonobo's life. As a result they have been nicknamed the hippy primates.

GROWING APE

While Jackie, an adult female orangutan, is busy feeding from bark and young, pinkish leaves, her shaggy-haired offspring, clinging to her long orange fur, slowly reaches out to the nearby branches. One hand first, then a foot, then a second hand. He is making his first steps in the tree-top world. But his mother, although still having her late lunch, keeps a close and constant watch over him. A 20-metre fall could be fatal and she vetoes each perilous initiative by grabbing her little daredevil and bringing him back 'home' by her side. He is six months old but it will be another year and a half before he begins to trail through the canopy, requiring his mother's help only to cross large gaps. It is only after his fifth birthday that he will gradually become autonomous, although still always accompanying his mother. Even by the age of ten, the now independent orangutan will frequently pay visits to his

Learning to be a great ape

mother and travel with her for a few days. Learning to be a great ape is not an easy task and orangutans, gorillas, bonobos and chimpanzees have the longest childhood of any primate, and one of the longest among mammals. Having a large brain is firstly costly in terms of the body's various chemical processes, and requires a long maturation period to become fully operational. Secondly, the ape's 'survival instruction book' is closer to an encyclopaedia than a simple leaflet,

Etumbe turned out to be a perfect mother even though she had spent over a decade in a small cage in a medical lab before arriving at the Lola Ya Bonobo sanctuary.

and it takes between five and eight years for the young ape to acquire all the skills, knowledge and competences of his species. In these first years, the mother plays a crucial role. As well as her role as protector and nurse, she also supervises and participates in the apprenticeship of her offspring. Orangutans not only live in the slow lane, they also have a mainly solitary existence. The young stay with their mothers, from whom they learn everything. For this reason, a mother orangutan only gives birth to one offspring, doing so every five to seven years,

Each individual ape has his own character which is developed during childhood and linked to his mother's personality. If some are calm, playful, jealous or jokey, others are more timid, aggressive, courageous or curious.

"The young orangutan is tied to his mother by an invisible rubber band."

and a remarkable bond unites them, the longest and most intense among mammals. As primatologist Carel van Schaik explains, "the older sibling is not completely

independent even after the new baby is born: it will travel through the forest as if tied to its mother by an invisible rubber band". She is so thoughtful and dedicated that she will make detours to specific trees solely to enable her offspring to feed on flowers (the first solid food they ingest before moving to a fruit diet), make bridges between tree-gaps with her own body, and bend branches toward him so he can reach some fruity delicacies. Moreover, during her offspring's first months of life the mother changes her sleeping habits and avoids building her night nest too close to a fruiting tree – usually quite a practical choice as, in the morning, she can have breakfast in bed. But frugivores concentrate there, and attract predators too, specially at night. The bond is so strong that a mother orangutan will defend her offspring whatever happens, even in the face of poachers who will kill her in order to

capture her baby, which is destined for the pet trade. But early infant care and the mother-offspring relationship is no less important in more social ape species such as the bonobo, the gorilla and the chimpanzee, although some other members of the group may also take part in the young ape's

apprenticeship. The infant ape will watch closely everything his mother and other adults are doing. When he begins to change from his mother's milk to solid food, he will only taste what she is eating and will slowly learn the basic menu of the species. Unlike monkeys, it is not only a matter of individual learning, but as primatologist Tetsuro Matsuzawa explains, "an education by master-apprenticeship in which the mother and elder members in the group show the model. Infants have a strong motivation to copy adults mastering a task, and they in return are highly tolerant towards the apprentice". In Bossou, Guinea, where Tetsuro Matsuzawa conducts field research, infant chimpanzees

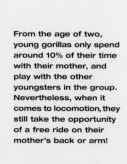

From the age of two, young gorillas only spend around 10% of their time with their mother, and play with the other youngsters in the group. Nevertheless, when it comes to locomotion, they still take the opportunity of a free ride on their mother's back or arm!

At Ape school, the mother plays the teacher's role

are totally fascinated by the nut-cracking behaviour of the adults; they observe them intensely and occasionally grab a piece of the highly nutritious almond they have just opened. By allowing this, the adults "encourage the young ones to continue their apprenticeship", notes Tetsuro Matsuzawa. This can go even further with the mother helping her offspring to crack a nut open, as Christophe Boesch observed in the Taï chimpanzee community in Ivory Coast. But learning is a long process, especially for some complex behaviours such as co-operative hunting which, according to Christophe Boesch, is the most difficult technique to master and requires three decades of apprenticeship. This is followed by panda nut opening and an intensive 13- to 14-year course in cracking. The importance of the mother-offspring bond is not limited to apprenticeship, but is closely linked to psychological development and construction of the infant's personality. In more than four

decades of research at Gombe National Park
in Tanzania, Jane Goodall observed that
young chimpanzees with very affectionate
and supportive mothers grow up as calm
individuals, showing confidence in themselves, whereas those raised by careless
and stressed mothers are more likely to
develop a hyperactive, impatient and nervous
character, and are unable to build up stable
relationships. This highlights the importance
of very early experience, similar to that
which has been observed in human children.
In the lush, tangled vegetation of the almost

Japanese researchers
long ago recognised
that each ape had his
own personnality. It is
because some will be
more curious than others
that new behaviours can
emerge and be adopted
by the community, leading
to new traditions and
cultures.

Learning to be an acrobat is not an easy task, and this young Sumatran orangutan still travels clinging to his mother.

impenetrable Bwindi forest, two infant gorillas are playing hide-and-seek behind some wild celery plants. Suddenly, they discover a large rotten trunk where giant ants are crawling. The first ape lets one insect climb onto his forearm and then eats the sweet delicacy. The second, having observed the scene closely, tries as well but once it is on his hairy arm, the ant disappears. The little gorilla desperately inspects his fur, but in vain. Suddenly I see him jump with surprise, as the ant reappears on his foot. After having caught the insect, he joins his

Professor **Christophe Boesch**, Director of the Max-Planck Institute for Evolutionary Anthropology in Leipzig, says, "In the Taï chimpanzee community, the mother relies on pedagogy to help and stimulate her offspring's acquisition of the nut-cracking technique. She will provide him with certain elements and a chance to practise, such as leaving the hammer she is using behind on the anvil while collecting more nuts. But she can also teach him some aspects of the task. In one case, a chimpanzee mother replaced a panda nut properly on the anvil, after her 6-year old son had incorrectly positioned it. In another case, a mother showed her 4-year old daughter how to hold the hammer, by turning it very slowly and conspicuously into the correct position, and she kept this grip while cracking a few nuts in front of her. In both cases, the mother interrupted what she was doing to help her offspring. Such teaching occurrences are very rare, even in humans, outside the school system."

friends and they play wrestling until their respective mothers call them to order. Such scenes are common and are part of the apprenticeship, and even the adults sometimes join in the game! Through play you get to know your peers, how to behave with them, and the limits you should not cross, and you also experience the rules of hierarchy in the group. By playing, some infants also become inventors, like Jeje, a young chimpanzee in Bossou, who had been mastering ant-dipping for safari ants

While playing, young apes learn the social codes of the community and how to behave in the group. They also discover their environment, like Kikwit (top), a little bonobo who got fascinated by water plants making a 'plop' noise when squeezed.

on the ground since he was four. By then, he had also started to use the stick tool to collect arboreal ants that had never been fished or eaten by the members of the community before, as Tetsuro Matsuzawa explains. At first the stick Jeje used to capture the ants was exactly the same length as the ground safari ant tool used by the group. However, three years later, when he was seven years old, he shortened the tool by 15cm, transforming it into a more effective tree-ant fishing stick. Will this invention be lost, or adopted by others and eventually become a cultural behaviour? No one can yet say.

DO APES APE?

Recognizing oneself in a mirror, pretending to be blind or hidden while playing with another of the species, tricks, deception and Machiavellian behaviour are all cognitive abilities that were once, wrongly, thought to be unique to humans.

Outside, it is snowing delicate white petals.
It's the cherry blossom season in Japan.
But Aï is so taken up by her task that she
doesn't seem to notice. Her large hairy hand
touches the numbers displayed randomly
on a computer and puts them back into
sequential order so fast I can hardly keep
up with her. Aï is a 30-year-old chimpanzee
living at the Inuyama Primate Research
Institute. After each correct answer she
receives not a treat but a 100 yen coin.
Aï waits until she has got two or three of
these and then goes to the other side of the

experimental booth, to a vending machine
which distributes raisins, apple pieces and
peanuts. The fascinating fact is that Pandesa,
another female, waits until she has about
20 coins in her hand before she spends
them on food. Can we see in this behaviour
the roots of the human economic system?
This cognitive experiment is fascinating, but
it is only one among many. Slowly, the gap
between humans and the other primates,
built up by philosophers and scientists,
narrows as we discover that apes are able
to recognize themselves in a mirror – a sign

"The study of primate cognition dates back to Charles Darwin and Georges Romanes. In the late seventies there was another boom with the study of "ape language" as a result of the cognitive revolution which cognitive ethology sprang from with Donald Griffin's work. Study on Xenophobia is documenting whether bonobos and chimpanzees have different physiological and/or behavioral responses to the sound of strangers or familiar individuals. We were so surprised when two groups of bonobos simply had sex and played when reunited after a two-year separation. This is absolutely an impossibility with chimps. Now the question is whether we find the signature of this difference in their physiology."
Brian Hare & Vanessa Woods, Hominoid Psychology Research Group, Max Planck Institute for Evolutionary Anthropology, Leipzig.

If chimpanzees are hyperactive and a bit disorderly when it comes to completing a task, orangutans seem to think the problem through first before even trying to resolve it, and hence usually achieve success at the first attempt. When rain pours down, they make themselves little umbrellas from leaves.

All great apes smile and laugh, but sometimes, as with this chimpanzee (right), a forced laugh with bared teeth can indicate fear and uneasiness.

of a sort of self-consciousness – and to manufacture and use tools or learn a symbolic or sign language. It all began in the 1960s when Jane Goodall witnessed a chimpanzee removing leaves from a twig and carefully inserting it into a termite mound. Then, the chimpanzee took out the tool and sucked up all the insects that had grabbed

An amazing Ape's tool kit

the intruding object. Since then the great ape tool kit has expanded with, for example, twigs placed under their feet by Liberian chimpanzees, held between the toes like flip-flops, and used to climb up the spiny trunks of kapok trees; or the use of wooden claws by orangutans in Sumatra to open hard-shelled cemengang fruits. It has long been known that great apes in captivity have huge cognitive skills. Wolfgang Köhler reported

in the 1920s that the chimpanzees he was taking care of were piling up wooden boxes and using branches to get hold of bananas tied up so high they were out of reach for non-tool-using individuals. A few years ago, I visited the language research centre in Atlanta and stood face to face with Kanzi, a male bonobo, only separated from him by a wire mesh. He took his symbol board and began to 'talk' asking me to 'play chase' with him. I was mesmerised and puzzled: I seemed to be facing a mirror but the reflection was no longer of a wild beast driven by instinct, but one of our own humanity. The French writer Rabelais had of course never encountered a great ape when he wrote in the 15th century that a laugh was the defining characteristic of man, yet I have seen bono-bos tickle themselves and split their sides laughing. Today, it is recognised that we are all one family, since we are great apes too.

THE CULTURAL APES

Crack! crack! crack!... The forest resonates with the sound of hammering. Black shadows thread their way stealthily through the large tree trunks in front of us. Chimpanzees! The narrow path leads us to a small clearing on top of mount Gban, overlooking the village of Bossou in Guinea. And here, in the cocoon-like atmosphere of an early morning, accompanied by a colourful bird concert, a group of chimpanzees is sitting, busily splitting open palm oil nuts with stones. They use a stone hammer and an anvil, sometimes adding a wedge to prevent the nut from sliding away before the final blow

According to primatologist William McGraw, a culture can be defined as "the way we do things". Chimpanzees display 39 cultural behaviours such as nut-cracking in Guinea (left) and some are even reproduced in captivity like the use of fishing tools in the Singapore zoo's chimpanzees.

Tetsuro Matsuzawa and
his research team have
been studying the Bossou
chimpanzees in Guinea
since 1986. There, they
use a variety of tools,
such as stone hammers
and anvils to crack open
palm nuts, or sponge-
leaves folded in their
mouth like origami to
collect water hidden in
hollow tree trunks.

"*The cultural behaviour study of the great apes brought a change to the basic attitude towards conservation. It demonstrated that each ape community may have a behavioural, cognitive, or social character that is unique. Therefore, we shouldn't proclaim conservation priority zones simply based on the estimated number of ape individuals in them. As each species is unique, so is the community and the individual. For example, Bossou in Guinea has only a group of 12 chimpanzees. Is it meaningless to protect such a tiny population? Definitely NOT. It is so important because of the 30 years accumulation of knowledge about the community, and because of the unique tradition of it.*"
Tetsuro Matsuzawa, *Professor of the Language and Intelligence Section, Primate Research Institute of Kyoto University, Japan.*

– a further indication of technical ability. This is a true stone workshop, probably comparable to those of early *Homo abilis*. Interestingly, here as well as further south in the Taï forest in Ivory Coast, chimpanzees are really wild about nuts. They are less so outside these two communities, even though palm oil, coula or panda nuts may be available. Such behavioural variations convinced researchers that great apes have, like humans, traditions and cultures. Another of the huge barriers between Man and Animal has fallen although, for Frans de Waal, "the question of whether animals have cultures is like asking whether chickens can fly". However this was not a new idea since in the 1950's Japanese scientists were already talking about cultures after witnessing Imo,

All apes have an aversion/fascination relationship to water. Orangutans usually avoid rivers, swamps and other liquid surfaces, but not this reintroduced female (right). In Tanjung Puting National Park, this young red ape drinks from pitcher plants, using them as cups.

a female Japanese macaque on Koshima island, washing sweet potatoes in the sea. This culinary habit then spread among the group and is now part of the community's social repertoire. But in Japanese society there has never been such a nature vs culture duel as in the western world, where it is driven by Cartesian rationalism. There lies the difference in the way we see our closest relatives and our place in the natural world. Researchers working on

Imo's cuisine class, Japanese society and Cartesian rationalism

chimpanzees in Africa made an inventory of all their tool technology and social customs, and concluded that about 40 behaviours appeared to be cultural variations. Since then we keep discovering new cultural patterns and behaviours, not only in chimpanzees but also in orangutans and probably in gorillas too. If genes determine the general abilities and behavioural repertoire of the species, as they do in humans, it is nevertheless inconceivable that they tell

primates exactly how to crack open a nut, make a leaf napkin or learn the movement of the rain dance of the Ugandan chimpanzees of Kibale. And non-genetic transmission of habits is what culture is all about. Individual innovation is crucial, as well as social transmission of the newly-invented behaviour from one generation to the next. And this is where the social life of great apes comes into play. Most traditions are acquired through social learning: mastering the nutcracking technique requires from 3.5 to 5 years of intense observation of experienced tool users by the young apprentice, as well as many

trials and many more errors smashing the nut or missing it completely. And how can one learn the grooming hand clasp ritual, an elegant, mutual gesture observed in Mahale (Tanzania) and Kibale (Uganda)? In the Bossou community, two adult females, Pama and Nin, who emigrated after the critical learning period from a non-nutcracking group, have never succeeded in the task, although their offspring did, after being in contact with the other members of the group since birth. And what about solitary orangutans? They also entered the select culture club once primatologists discovered that the

frequently-grouping Sumatran Suaq
population was using many tools to gain
access for example to cemengang fruits,
hidden behind a hard shell covered with
razor-sharp whiskers; the neighbouring
Ketambe population, on the eastern side
of the Gunung Leuser National Park did not
use tools, although the same fruits were
present and eaten. Great apes have opened
up a new era of animal behaviour studies,
where nature has come to terms with culture
and where researchers now recognize the
existence of ape individuals with their own
personalities and characters.

In contrast to orangutans,
bonobos love water and
in the Lola Ya Bonobo
Sanctuary the daily bath
cannot be ignored or
skipped (above). This
female chimpanzee in
Gabon (below) doesn't
bother herself with
drinking cups or other
such devices.

Pl. IV.

Prince Joseph en tenue de soirée. Ce chimpanzé, qui fit les
délices du public des music-halls, a été dressé par M. Joyat,
l'un des professeurs de l'illustre Consul (p. 61)

OF APES AND MEN

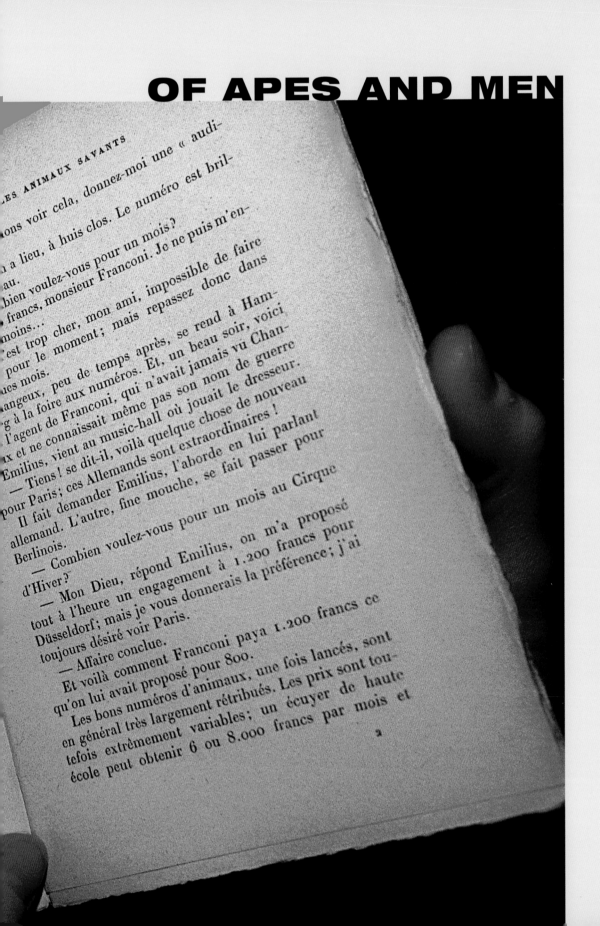

LES ANIMAUX SAVANTS

...ons voir cela, donnez-moi une « audi-
...a lieu, à huis clos. Le numéro est bril-
...au.
...bien voulez-vous pour un mois?
...francs, monsieur Franconi. Je ne puis m'en-
...moins...
...'est trop cher, mon ami, impossible de faire
...pour le moment; mais repassez donc dans
...es mois.

...angeux, peu de temps après, se rend à Ham-
...g à la foire aux numéros. Et, un beau soir, voici
...l'agent de Franconi, qui n'avait jamais vu Chan-
...x et ne connaissait même pas son nom de guerre
Emilius, vient au music-hall où jouait le dresseur.

— Tiens! se dit-il, voilà quelque chose de nouveau
pour Paris; ces Allemands sont extraordinaires !

Il fait demander Emilius, l'aborde en lui parlant
allemand. L'autre, fine mouche, se fait passer pour
Berlinois.

— Combien voulez-vous pour un mois au Cirque
d'Hiver?

— Mon Dieu, répond Emilius, on m'a proposé
tout à l'heure un engagement à 1.200 francs pour
Düsseldorf; mais je vous donnerais la préférence; j'ai
toujours désiré voir Paris.

— Affaire conclue.

Et voilà comment Franconi paya 1.200 francs ce
qu'on lui avait proposé pour 800.

Les bons numéros d'animaux, une fois lancés, sont
en général très largement rétribués. Les prix sont tou-
tefois extrêmement variables; un écuyer de haute
école peut obtenir 6 ou 8.000 francs par mois et

January 31st 1961, Cape Canaveral. At the
NASA laboratory, the Mercury space capsule
is about to be launched with the first
astronaut on board, named Ham. But Ham,
which stands for Holloman Aero Med, is not
an ordinary spaceman, he is a chimpanzee.
Along with 64 others, taken from their

African forest home while they were still
babies, Ham was trained to pilot the capsule
via a system of punishments (electric
impulses) and rewards (sweets). The effects
of weightlessness and radiation were still
unknown, so why risk the life of a human
astronaut when chimpanzees were so skilful

and could perform the task? After his successful space flight, Ham was acclaimed a hero and was even granted the honour of the cover of Life magazine. The success of Enos – another chimponaut – was even more astonishing; while the capsule was in orbit, a fuel leak caused it to veer off course and the punishment-reward system was reversed. Nevertheless, Enos carried on the manœuvres he knew were correct and succeeded in bringing the capsule back to earth despite the electric shocks he received. The researchers were even more surprised that they failed to reproduce Enos' actions. Real heroes of the conquest of space, Ham, Enos and the other chimponauts did not retire to a pleasant sanctuary, but ended up in medical laboratories in conditions of isolation and suffering. Close cousins when we need their help, apes become mere guinea-pigs for science, devoid of feelings,

Although they are worshipped, the ever shrinking forest habitat of the Bossou chimpanzees has led them to help themselves frequently in the fields, leading to conflicts with the humans.

A tumultuous and ambiguous relationship...

when it comes to ethics. Since their discovery by the western world, during the Age of the Enlightenment, the great apes have been in turn clowns, guinea-pigs and, more widely, a source of profit. Man both denigrates and exploits this resemblance between himself and the great apes. When the first great ape bowed to a cabaret audience in tails and top hat, undoubtedly a gust of philosophical wind blew through the onlookers. But the battle to recognize our kinship still had a long way to go. One of the most memorable oratorical encounters took place in June 1860

in Oxford, and brought together Bishop Samuel Wilberforce and anthropologist and anatomist Thomas Henry Huxley. Wilberforce, violently against Darwin's Origin of Species and seeking to score a point against Darwin's disciples, asked Huxley whether he would prefer to think of himself as descended from an ape on his grandfather's or grand-mother's side. And Huxley, Darwin's defender, is said to have answered that he was not ashamed of his ancestry, but that he would be ashamed to be connected to a man who used great gifts to obscure the truth. He concluded that he would rather have an ape for an ancestor than a bishop. If apes and humans are indeed too close for comfort

A chimpanzee skull is
carefully kept by the two
Bossou village founders'
families and everyone likes
to bow down to ask for
help, advice or forgiveness
in front of this totem
representing their ancestor.

in the western world, elsewhere, especially in the apes' home territory, the relationship between apes and men is much less equivocal. The Mendes inhabiting the Guinean forest call the chimpanzees the 'Numu gbahamisia', different beings, coming from the same ancestral population as humans, the 'Huan nasia ta lo a ngoo', those 'animals who walk on two feet'. In other African villages, apes

King Kong and Man's desire to break off the link with his animality

are buried next to humans to signify the close kinship. In the village of Bossou in southern Guinea, chimpanzees are the totems of the two founder families of the village, who consider the apes to be their ancestors, and worship and protect them. Far from refusing this kinship, most Africans living close to the great apes know that indeed they are bright, live in complex societies, make and use tools and hunt like humans do. Even after a century of questioning nourished by growing research in the field, we still feel uncomfortable about our ape ancestors, an ambivalent kinship which is the theme of many books, essays, films and sculptures. Man is still far from ready to give up his top position in the long-established *Scala naturae*.

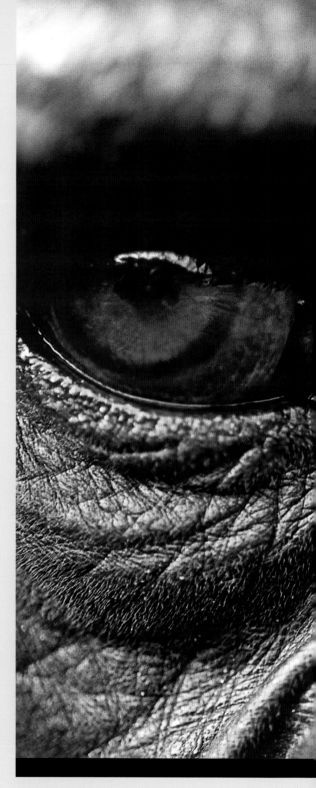

Face to face, eye to eye
... so much humanity is
contained in a bonobo's
glance.

GHBOURS OR ENEMIES?

In the hot, moist atmosphere of an early
equatorial afternoon, leaning against the huge
buttress roots of a Meranti and overlooking
a fig tree, I am fascinated by the never-ending
ballet of mammals, birds and other animals
coming to gorge themselves. It is fruit-
shortage season now in the Bornean
rainforest but not for figs, which provide
abundant calories and therefore form a highly
desirable staple diet for all animals around.
Everyone has made an appointment at
the fig-bar and while Mono, a young male
orangutan, gobbles up fruit after fruit, and
hornbills come and go, a gibbon sits in

The Congo Basin, the second largest tropical forest after the Amazon rainforest, hosts a vast number of primate species including the Angolan colobus, and the rare and fascinating drills (far left) and mandrills, both of which are forest baboons.

Jason Mier, chimpanzee activist and independent investigator, says: "Take a country like the DRC, with likely the largest population of chimpanzees. It is ranked as one of the most corrupt in the world and the political situation makes it nearly impossible to work on the ground. Logging has now been opened up in a major way: more than 150 contracts between the government and logging companies are now covering an area of tens of millions of hectares. Many of these contracts are semi-legal at best, and very little of the taxes which this logging is supposed to bring in are ever collected. There are new Ministerial decrees giving prices for the capture of chimpanzees, gorillas and bonobos, as well as hunting prices for many other allegedly fully protected species. This should not be seen as one country where there are the most extreme problems, but representative of central Africa as a whole – widespread corruption, expanding logging, and unabated hunting."

a corner having a late breakfast while an armada of squirrels of various sizes and colours settles down round the table too. Grunts arise from below. It's a bearded pig, taking advantage of all the left-overs thrown down by guests in the canopy. Everyone is living under the same canopy-roof as the apes, although competition for highly desirable food can occur in periods of scarcity. In the Taï forest in Ivory Coast (as in all the other communities), chimpanzees

In central Africa, apes face two major threats: deforestation for the timber industry – right, a barge filled with tree trunks moves down the Congo river – and bushmeat hunting. These decorated gorilla skulls (above) from Cameroon were confiscated by French customs officials.

In the Sumatran
rainforests, apes,
Sumatran rhinoceros,
Thomas' leaf monkeys
and crab-eating
macaques live under
the same canopy-roof.

In complete silence, once a colobus has been spotted in the foliage, one ape climbs up and pushes the prey in front of him towards another ape who has anticipated the direction of the colobus, while the rest of the troupe follows on the ground. But the colobus has developed an anti-predation strategy as well – although it isn't 100% foolproof – by associating with Diana monkeys. These forest gossips are small but always on the alert, and they have learned to decipher the apes' vocalisations and run for their lives

A crime against biodiversity

to the very thinnest branches when danger is sensed. Whether relationships with neighbours are peaceful or agitated, the apes live in a complex web of life where all species are entangled. While I was in Borneo studying orangutans, I flew in a helicopter over the broccoli-like roof of the emerald forest. Flying in this giant, metallic insect was thrilling: it offered the same view as that of the great hornbill, loudly hovering over the monochromatic, yet not monotonous, chlorophyll-coloured ocean. But suddenly, this green Eden revealed some large reddish scars – logging roads looking like veins through which the forest is bleeding to death. Deforestation is a cancer eating away the silvan paradise and a crime against biodiversity. Each year, 7.3 million hectares are lost to palm oil or rubber tree plantations, paper mills, timber exploitation or coltan,

are not such friendly neighbours. Meat is on their menu and they hunt small mammals, birds, frogs and frequently other primates, such as the colobus. If, in Tanzania's Gombe, hunting is mostly a lone enterprise, in Taï chimpanzees hunt in highly organised and co-ordinated groups: they co-operate.

gold or oil extraction. In less than a century, more than half the forest cover has disappeared. This loss of habitat is the most significant threat to apes and to their neighbours, whether primates, beetles, amphibians, flowers or birds. Chimpanzees probably numbered more than a million in the 1960's, but today there are a mere 150,000. There were 100,000 bonobos in 1980 and two decades have reduced their numbers to 10 to 20,000, and gorillas have declined dramatically lately, partly due to Ebola virus epidemics and to poaching. With fewer than 5,000 individuals, the Sumatran

More than 75% of the Indonesian forest cover has already disappeared due to the timber industry, monocultures and large shrimp farms, and the wildlife trade is a by-product of this deforestation.

orangutan is the most threatened ape species, while Bornean orangutans number about 40 to 50,000 but are constantly declining, as are gibbons and siamangs. Today all ape species are on the brink of extinction, and this is the responsibility of *Homo sapiens*, who contrary to his name is far from wise, but greedy and attracted by short-term profit. Worse, opening new tracks into the dense and impenetrable forest brings new dangers from poaching and the bushmeat trade. Once the only meat resource for remote villages in the African Congo basin, bushmeat has lately become a fashionable dish in cities, the caviar of an African elite. Meanwhile new logging roads enable poachers to penetrate further and further into formerly inaccessible areas, and logging trucks too often become public

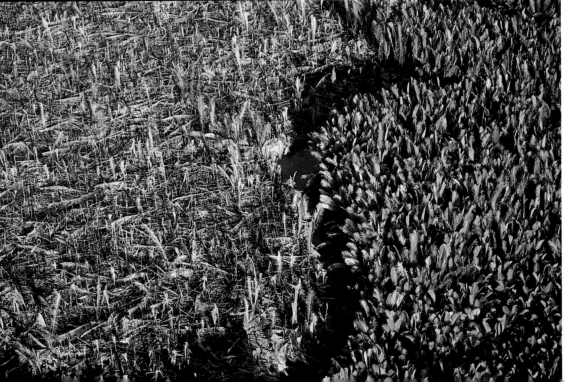

In Borneo and Sumatra, millions of hectares of rainforest are burned and converted to large-scale monocultures. Today, the survival of orangutans is linked to the wood and paper industry and to oil palm, a product exported throughout the world and used everywhere, from cosmetics to the food industry or even in so-called 'bio' fuels.

buses for poachers, giving them and their kill a ride. But apes are also victims of the pet trade. As Jason Mier, a chimpanzee activist, explains, "The majority of this smuggling is done by an elite with connections, and more and more there seems to be a direct link with drug smugglers and human traffickers through a mafia-type organization". In Borneo and Sumatra, each year hundreds of baby orangutans are captured, after their protecting mother has been killed. Some are then smuggled out of Indonesia, and end up in bars, brothels or amusement parks to lure tourists and customers. Only one out of five usually survives.

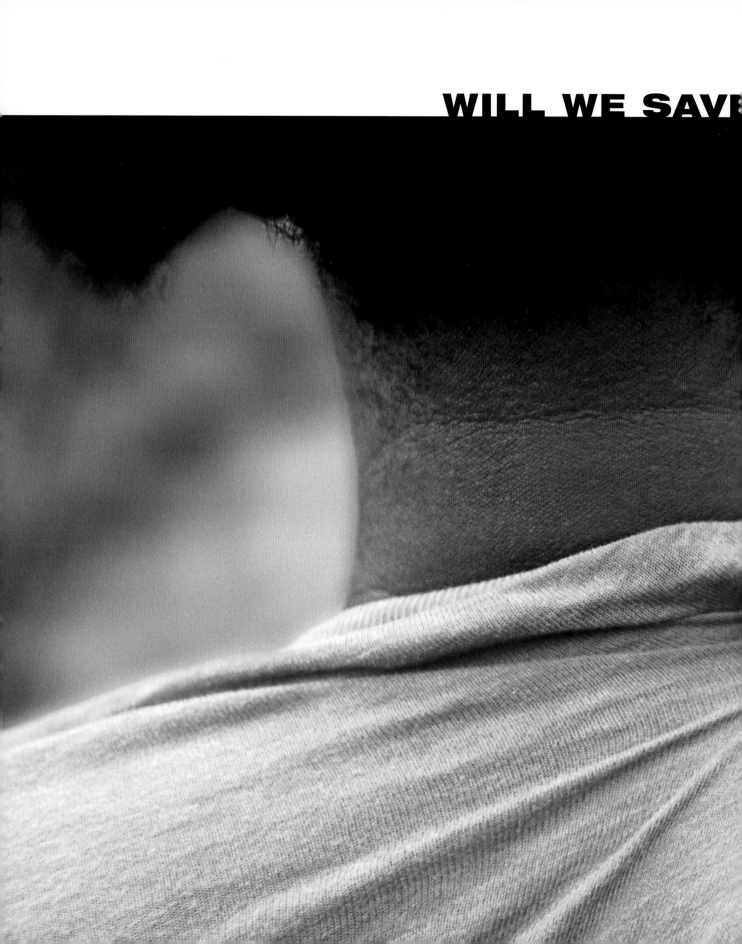

WILL WE SAVE

A pair of round, ebony-coloured eyes fixes an unblinking gaze on me, while an almost childlike hand reaches out through the cage's bars, begging for some tenderness. We are at the Kenya Wildlife Service in Nairobi, where six young chimpanzees have just arrived after being confiscated by airport customs officials. Arrived from Egypt, they were heading for Lagos, Nigeria, one of the most important illegal wildlife trade centres. Since then, these little hairy guys have been transferred to a sanctuary, and will be integrated into a social group of other orphaned chimpanzees. These rehabilitation

Ape refugees are more and more numerous due to accelerating deforestation. They find a safe haven in rehabilitation centres and sanctuaries such as Bakoumba in Gabon for the chimpanzees (left) or Lola Ya Bonobo (right) in the Democratic Republic of the Congo.

and re-introduction centres have flourished since the 1960s, both in south-east Asia and in Africa. They are a direct result of the work of Non-Governmental Organisations (NGOs) with legal authority to confiscate smuggled and illegally kept or captured apes. The problem is that even in well-documented cases, in which the national and international laws concerning the protection of endangered species such as the great apes have been blatantly disregarded, there is seldom any prosecution or penalty. The illegal wildlife trade is quite a safe business to get involved in, for the hunters themselves, the officials in Africa who deliver false permits, the airline employees who close their eyes to some of

Claudine André, founder and president of Lola Ya Bonobo sanctuary and of 'Les Amis des Bonobos du Congo', notes, "The bonobos in the sanctuary have become ambassadors for their species. They help educate the population, and develop a better understanding of wildlife and the reasons it must be protected. Education is a first and crucial step towards conservation. Last year, half of the orphans who arrived at Lola were given spontaneously by their (illegal) owners, and 30% in 2004 and 2005, a sign that the message we are giving is spreading. Internationally, the media also play an important role in mobilising efforts to save the great apes, and more widely the planet's biodiversity. If we fail to save our close cousins from extinction, I fear for the other species as well. I am afraid that one day, Man will be left alone face to face with himself."

The mother-infant bond is crucial, so at the Lola Ya Bonobo Sanctuary, human substitute mothers, like Henriette, take care of the orphans, usually as if they were their own child, bringing them back to life through the building of a close and tender relationship.

**Ape refugee camps
have flourished since the 1960s
and host hundreds of orphans**

The confiscated gibbons will eventually be reintroduced on safe forested islands by the Kalaweit project (left). Malou, a young female bonobo (right) was discovered in Roissy airport, France, on her way to Russia. Confiscated from the traffickers, she was sent back to the Democratic Republic of the Congo and the Lola Ya Bonobo Sanctuary.

the wildlife shipments, or the buyers – private owners, pet shops and sometimes even so-called zoos. But, explains Jason Mier, "for every problem, there is a solution: we can all choose not to go to zoos or circuses which use apes, not to stay in hotels which have young apes for the souvenir photo business, nor use airlines involved in wildlife smuggling, while making known the reasons we choose not to fly with them".

The bushmeat trade is another problem. But, ironically, Ebola disease could help the apes, although many have already died from this haemorrhagic fever in the last few years. It has been demonstrated that humans can contract Ebola while handling or eating infected apes, a fact that could contribute to the reduction of a trade that is driven more by profit than by the needs of subsistence. Further, alternative protein sources are slowly being developed in central Africa, including fish farming, and cane rat and red river hogs breeding for example. Helped by an NGO, some hunters have moved into bee-keeping projects to meet a growing demand for honey, while some have become research assistants

in behavioural and ecological field projects, or ecoguards and specialized wildlife guides. However, the top priority is to preserve the last remaining tropical and equatorial rainforests and the wild ape populations that depend on them. Two goals need to be achieved simultaneously: stopping the ongoing and

It is all about changing consumption habits

large-scale deforestation, and ensuring the total preservation and sustainable use of the remaining fragments of forest in Borneo, Sumatra and West Africa and in the still largely untouched Congo Basin. Not an easy task – indeed it looks much like David versus Goliath – but most products that come out of or derive from the forests – hardwood, palm oil, diamonds, coltan, paper pulp – are destined mainly for western markets; it is therefore our responsibility to change these consumption habits. We should reject tropical woods and by-products that are not certified by the Forest Stewardship Council, the only label that ensures environmental and social criteria for the sustainable use of the tropical forests, and avoid products which are linked to deforestation. There is still a long way to go before all those ape refugees can live safely again in a beautiful and preserved forest.

Protecting the last wild apes is a priority and in west Africa it goes also through building green corridors such as the Wild Chimpanzee Foundation initiatives, linking the remaining forest islands.

From left to right, the photographer Cyril Ruoso surrounded by an adolescent chimpanzee (Gabon), a female orangutan (Borneo) and a male silverback mountain gorilla (Rwanda).

Rwanda, the land of a thousand hills.
In this tiny country, every patch of land is
used to grow potatoes, beans, and delicate
pyrethrum flowers which wave in the wind.
It is in the tattered forest, confined to the
highest areas of this miniature country,
that the remaining mountain gorillas live.
Escorted by half a dozen guards armed
with grenades and machine guns we climb
up the sticky, muddy and very slippery
slope. While struggling not to fall I cannot
help thinking of Rwanda's tormented history,
impregnated with the blood of genocide.
Central Africa is indeed a paradox: a lush,
Eden-like biodiversity on one side and
a deeply wounded country on the other.
Strangely, in this socially disrupted region,
nature has won one great victory:
the mountain gorillas have been saved, thanks
to the dedication of some humans. It has
been realised that the apes here are much

Ecotourism as a key to the anti-poaching battle

more valuable alive than dead, thanks to
ecotourism, which has been the key to the
anti-poaching battle both in Rwanda and
in Uganda. This example demonstrates that
giving a value to biodiversity can help protect
it. Today, a gorilla permit costs between
US$375 and US$500 per person for an hour
among the gentle giants. In the Bwindi
Ugandan National Park, ecotourism generates
around US$2 million a year, and provides

full-time employment for some 95 people.
Moreover, part of the benefit is coming
back to the neighbourhood through the
construction of infrastructure such as
roads, schools, community clinics, and also
through various tourism-linked activities
such as souvenir shops. But ecotourism
should result from the wish of the local
people, not from the unrestrained desire
of westerners for back-to-nature holidays.

Locals must be able to visit the parks as well, at a price they can afford to pay. Conservation and ecotourism must not be developed at no matter what cost. Conservation begins with education, as Claudine André from Lola Ya Bonobo says. Meeting and photographing apes in the wild is a deeply satisfying experience. But to respect the apes in their environment, you should be as discreet as possible when approaching them, and try to understand them. Basic rules should be respected at all times: first of all by being very careful about health issues, which means never getting too close to the apes, and by refraining from touching them. Since they are so genetically and anatomically close to us, transmission of disease is a real danger; a cold that is mild for humans could be fatal to apes. Likewise it is important not to feed them: if they get used to tourists providing food, they are likely to become aggressive with anyone who won't give them anything to eat. Ecotourism, be it in

Ecotourism in Rwanda on a misty day in the Parc National des Volcans.

A journey through humanity in the company of the apes

Africa or in South-East Asia, can help apes if it is well-managed, integrates the communities and preserves the apes from too many disturbances. They allow us to invade their privacy; let us reward them for the privilege by leaving no physical or psychological tracks behind!

Select Bibliography

Karl Ammann and Dale Peterson (2003) Eating apes. University of California Press.

Christophe Boesch and Hedwige Boesch-Achermann (2000) The chimpanzees of the Taï forest. Oxford University Press.

Richard Byrne (1995) The thinking ape, evolutionary origins of intelligence. Oxford University Press.

Julian Caldecott and Lera Miles, eds (2005) World atlas of great apes and their conservation. Prepared at the UNEP World Conservation Monitoring Centre. University of California Press.

Frans de Waal and Frans Lanting (1997) Bonobo: the forgotten ape. University of California Press.

Frans de Waal (2000) Chimpanzee politics: power and sex among apes. Johns Hopkins University Press.

Frans de Waal (2001) The ape and the sushi master. Cultural reflections of a primatologist. Basic Books.

Frans de Waal (2006) Our inner ape: the best and worst of human nature. Granta Books.

Dian Fossey (2000) Gorillas in the mist. Houghton Mifflin.

Biruté Galdikas (1995) Reflections of Eden: my life with the orangutans of Borneo. Indigo.

Jane Goodall (1986) The chimpanzees of Gombe, patterns of behaviour. Belknap Press of Harvard University Press.

Jane Goodall (1999) In the shadow of man. Phoenix.

Jane Goodall (2000) Through a window. Thirty years with the chimpanzees of Gombe. Phoenix.

Angelika Hofer, Michael Huffman and Gunther Ziesler (2000) Mahale: a photographic encounter with chimpanzees. Sterling Publishing.

Carole Jahme (2000) Beauty and the beasts: woman, ape and evolution. Virago.

William McGrew (1992) Chimpanzee material culture. Cambridge University Press.

William C. McGrew, Linda F Marchant and Toshisada Nishida (1996) Great ape societies. Cambridge University Press.

William McGrew (2004) The cultured chimpanzee: reflections on cultural primatology. Cambridge University Press.

Tetsuro Matsuzawa, Masaki Tomonaga and Masayuki Tanaka (2006). Cognitive development in chimpanzees. Springer Verlag.

Carel van Schaik (2004) Among orangutans. Red apes and the rise of human culture. Belknap Press of Harvard University Press.

Richard Wrangham and Dale Peterson (1996) Demonic males. Apes and the origins of human violence. Bloomsbury Publishing.

Acknowledgments

Producing a book is always a long journey, with numerous encounters, joys and disappointments. We have both been following apes for the last decade, Cyril through a photographic journey and myself first as a researcher and then as a conservationist and reporter, trying to bring the plight of the apes to the attention of the general public. We want to warmly thank Carel van Schaik, Tetsuro Matsuzawa, Christophe Boesch, Jason Mier, Brian Hare, Vanessa Woods, Frans de Waal and Claudine André, who very kindly gave their valuable points of view and research results on various aspects of great ape behaviour, cognition, evolution and conservation.

Many thanks also to l'ORTPN (Office Rwandais du Tourisme et des Parcs Nationaux), Bakoumba (Gabon), BOS (Bornean Orangutan Survival Foundation), Kalaweit (Indonesia), Lola Ya Bonobo (DRC), la Vallée des Singes (France) and to Acung (Bukit Lawang, Sumatra) for their help in the field with the apes.

Special thanks to Sabrina Krief, Claudine André and Marie-Claude Bomsel for their friendship and some parts of the journey we shared, to Ichal Misjan who guided me and helped me collect data during all those long months following the orangutans in Borneo for my PhD, and finally our gratitude to Christine Baillet and Alain Pons for their wonderful work on this book and to Marie-Claude Grundmann for her numerous re-readings.

We must also warmly thank Kikwit, Etumbe, Mono, Bento, Manono, Jackie and her son, Mbandaka, Maya and all the others – may they forgive us if we cannot name them all here – for having allowed us to share some intimate moments, so intense, full of surprises and discoveries and for having opened the doors to their worlds to us and taught us humility and respect.

OTHER

Wild things...

TITLES

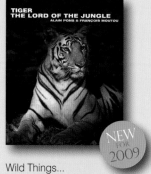

Wild Things...
Creatures of the Deep Blue
ISBN: 978-1-901268-31-7

Wild Things...
Gorillas
ISBN: 978-1-901268-35-5

Wild Things...
Tiger – The Lord of the Jungle
ISBN: 978-1-901268-40-9

Other wildlife titles published by

 **Evans Mitchell Books**

www.embooks.co.uk

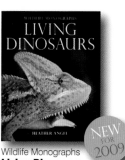

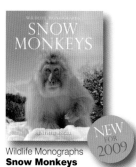

Wildlife Monographs
Snow Monkeys
ISBN: 978-1-901268-34-8

Wildlife Monographs
Living Dinosaurs
ISBN: 978-1-901268-36-2

Wildlife Monographs
Giant Pandas
ISBN: 978-1-901268-13-3

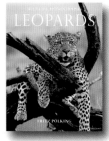

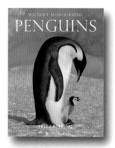

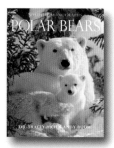

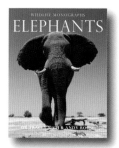

Wildlife Monographs
Loepards
ISBN: 978-1-901268-12-6

Wildlife Monographs
Sharks
ISBN: 978-1-901268-11-9

Wildlife Monographs
Penguins
ISBN: 978-1-901268-14-0

Wildlife Monographs
Polar Bears
ISBN: 978-1-901268-15-7

Wildlife Monographs
Elephants
ISBN: 978-1-901268-08-9

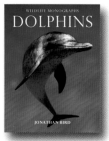

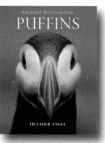

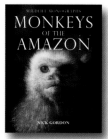

Wildlife Monographs
Dolphins
ISBN: 978-1-901268-17-1

Wildlife Monographs
Wolves
ISBN: 978-1-901268-18-8

Wildlife Monographs
Puffins
ISBN: 978-1-901268-19-5

Wildlife Monographs
Monkeys of the Amazon
ISBN: 978-1-901268-10-2

Wildlife Monographs
Cheetahs
ISBN: 978-1-901268-09-6